A City Divided
Ferguson & The George Floyd Protests

STEVEN PELLEGRINO

First paperback edition June 2023

ISBN 979-8-3992-6486-8

Book design by Steven Pellegrino

www.stevepellegrino.com

On August 9, 2014, Ferguson, Missouri, transformed from a little, unknown community in the Midwest to a global symbol of social injustice. For almost a year, there were protests in the St. Louis region. At that time, riots and protests decimated large portions of the city, resulting in millions of dollars in losses for primarily small businesses.

While neighboring North St. Louis County small towns were having trouble, Ferguson was bucking the trend with new companies and improvements to the neighborhood. Ferguson was a flourishing, expanding town that valued diversity before Michael Brown was shot in 2014; however, things changed afterward. The city's advancement came to a halt in 2014.

From 2014 to 2020, Ferguson city officials and residents worked to repair the city's image and reverse its deterioration as a result of outside activists after the shooting of Michael Brown. But over those six years, there were still protests in Ferguson while Black people were shot by police everywhere in the nation.

However, unlike the violent destruction Ferguson had previously witnessed, most protests were only inconvenient to the neighborhood. That lasted up to George Floyd's murder in May 2020 in Minneapolis. This event occurred over a month in 2020. Ferguson has many stories to tell, but this one is significant.

Following the shooting of Michael Brown in August 2014, Ferguson, Missouri, was depicted by the media as the most racist city in the country. Residents of the city, who took pleasure in being a varied, inviting community distinct from the larger St. Louis metro region where racial divisiveness has always persisted, were outraged by this fabricated label. The locals believed outside influences attempted to split the city to further their ends racially. In 2020, there were roughly 69 percent Black people and 22 percent White people. There wasn't a separate Ferguson for Blacks and Whites. Together, Black and White residents enjoyed the events and connected with their neighborhood by attending the twice-monthly summer concerts, the yearly charity Twilight Run, and the weekly farmer's market.

All the emotions from 2014 erupted once more in response to the murder of George Floyd. Over those six years, the advancements the city made quickly vanished.

After the destruction in 2014, when businesses were looted and burned down, many rebuilt and started over. Other businesses left. Ferguson had a reputation for being a community where a protest could begin anytime. People from outside Ferguson refrained from visiting shops and eateries; as a result, forcing businesses to close.

The Teakwood Shop, a barbershop that had been a mainstay in Ferguson for more than 55 years, was the first of three venerable businesses to close in 2017. The business window displayed several placards, one of which said, "Business is Closed for Retirement." Unfortunately, using retirement as an excuse was simpler than explaining the real cause of the store's closure.

Teakwood Shop owner Marty Buchheit quoted in the St. Louis/Southern Illinois Labor Tribune newspaper: *"I don't know how much longer I can hold out. Older people, my clientele, are already up in years, and they just aren't coming to Ferguson anymore. Every shopkeeper on the street is in the same boat. People aren't milling around in the daytime like they used to, and some are staying away from Ferguson completely."*

Ferguson Hardware was owned by Kim Taylor, who decided to shut down her family business a few months later. Ferguson Hardware was located 100 feet across the shared parking lot from The Teakwood Shop. The St. Louis Post-Dispatch quoted Taylor saying, *"There's just not enough business."*

Over 50 years have passed since the founding of Ferguson Hardware. Taylor owns the structure, and as of this writing in 2023, it is still up for sale.

Ferguson Optical, another long-standing member of the neighborhood, was located just 450 feet up the path connecting The Teakwood Shop and Ferguson Hardware.

Before the Floyd protests in January 2020, they closed their Ferguson location and moved their operations to Hazelwood, Missouri. No one has leased the Ferguson Optical shop more than three years later.

In 2023, after 83 years in Ferguson, the Fortune 500 Company Emerson Electric decided to leave Ferguson and relocate to Clayton, Missouri. Clayton is well known for its wealthy, educated, professional, and dual-income residents.

The Ferguson demonstrations against what happened to George Floyd were similar to those regarding Michael Brown. Owners of businesses boarded up the windows of their shops to lessen the harm caused by theft and fire. The city appears and feels deserted due to the businesses being boarded up. Protesters slowed down traffic on South Florissant Road in front of the Ferguson Police Department every evening. Graffiti was painted on the police department sign; several front windows were broken, and the building housing the Ferguson Police Department was vandalized. As the protests escalated, police were obliged to use riot smoke canisters and pepper balls to scatter the crowd.

Protesters spray-painted anti-cop graffiti on the pavement in front of the police station almost every evening. One evening, they also painted Black Lives Matter with white paint on the roadway in front of the station.

Handwritten "Black Owned" signs began to appear in storefront windows as owners of businesses saw their establishments looted once more and suffered additional losses due to arson. The placards warned protesters not to vandalize Black business owners' establishments in favor of attacking White and Asian-owned ones.

Professionally printed "Black Owned Business" placards that activists had paid for started to appear as the protests went on. Ferguson no longer had the unity it once did. Instead of standing with White and Asian business owners, Black business owners cultivated racial divisions. Frustrating to White business owners was the fact that they employed Black Ferguson residents.

The city saw a rise in tension. Residents who had previously been optimistic about their neighborhood now felt defeated. Many inhabitants, mostly senior White citizens, realized it was time to depart the neighborhood they cherished. After the riots in 2014 over Michael Brown, they stayed put. Instead, it took them six years to truly feel like they didn't belong in Ferguson.

Less than 13% of Ferguson's population is 65 and older. For Sale signs started to appear more frequently, and I started talking to my neighbors who were selling. They uttered the exact phrase, *"It's time."* Everyone I spoke with wanted to escape Ferguson and the St. Louis metropolitan region. They relocated to small rural, primarily White towns in Missouri.

Residents of color also felt frustrated. Protesters don't post a schedule of when they will shut down a street.

Because of this, many Black residents trying to get home would become stuck during a protester street closure and either go around or use the side streets. *"What's going on?"* they would yell out the windows of their vehicles. Many cars would shout back, *"But it has nothing to do with us,"* when a protester informed them they were denouncing George Floyd's death.

They were sympathetic, but they also understood that calling for police reform in Minneapolis, Minnesota, or bringing George Floyd justice would not be achieved by protests in Ferguson, Missouri.

The fact that Ferguson complied with every demand made by demonstrators and activists for six years—the majority of whom did not reside in Ferguson—long before the Floyd protests began- infuriated many locals.

- The Department of Justice and the city had signed a consent decree.
- The city reformed the courts.
- The city dismissed a large number of traffic tickets.
- The police force stopped pulling over vehicles and writing tickets.
- Over seven years, the city hired two new Black city managers to replace the departing White one.
- Thomas Jackson, a White police chief, resigned, but within five years, five Black police chiefs took his position.
- The city hired a Black city attorney after the White city attorney resigned.
- More Black candidates were elected to the city council by voters.
- Residents also chose the first Black mayor on June 2, 2020, as George Floyd protests took place.

For nine years, James Knowles presided as mayor of Ferguson. Knowles was the target of protesters who even attempted to have him recalled. But as he had already served three terms, he was no longer eligible to run.

Like the previous election, Knowles's last election, there were Black and White candidates. They both serve on the council for Ferguson. Because both candidates are women and Ferguson has never had a female mayor, the election would be crucial whether Ella Jones, a Black candidate, or Heather Robinett, a White candidate, won.

Ella Jones was chosen as Ferguson's first Black mayor, despite falling short of James Knowles in the last election three years prior.

A Black mayor is a result that many people desired but did not obtain three years earlier. However, on June 2, 2020, when #Ferguson was trending on Twitter, nobody mentioned this election. Instead, during the George Floyd protests, the media and online activists utilized #Ferguson to promote their anti-cop narrative and drive traffic to their websites. Social justice activists used the hashtag to gain followers by spreading any unfavorable information they could discover about Ferguson while ignoring the city's progress.

Media organizations and self-described activists on social media present themselves as being concerned about Ferguson. A successful outcome on election day doesn't suit the "us against them" narrative, but they still only care when there is something in it for them.

The citizens and the City of Ferguson have consistently collaborated to advance the interests of the entire city. One of the myths surrounding the demonstrations and the property damage is that the residents of Ferguson devastated their city.

But the truth was different.

Very few residents from Ferguson were involved in the unrest. Due to publicly available arrest records, we are aware of this. People looking to commit crimes saw an opportunity to do so by visiting Ferguson during a protest. The claim made by activists to their Twitter followers that they were "on the ground" in Ferguson when they had no relationship to the city other than to further a false narrative was likewise self-serving.

Meanwhile, local artists in the St. Louis area turned to their paintings as a form of activism as locals' resentment increased during the George Floyd protests. Artists congregated on South Florissant Road during the day to paint Black Lives Matter-related imagery on plywood panels covering storefront windows, the police station, and glass doors.

One artist, Ferguson resident Phil Berwick, painted small-scale signs affixed to a short stake and buried them in the dirt on several neighborhood streets. In contrast, other artists used a vulnerable community to spread their activism message.

The placards inquired about the well-being of those who lived on that street. The residents responded favorably to his gesture. No one has ever before inquired as to how the citizens of Ferguson were faring. Social media users and the media consistently presented the demonstrators as victims rather than as everyday people going about their daily lives.

When the George Floyd demonstrations in Ferguson ended, the demonstrators had not improved the situation for the locals or the city. Instead, millions of dollars were lost by innocent business owners as a result of theft, fire, and property damage. Employees and business owners of color lost their jobs and income. Additionally, the protests finally convinced many longtime residents to leave the city.

Residents of the St. Louis metro area still hold Ferguson in low regard. Storefronts remain vacant, property prices continue to be below the county average, and Ferguson's quality of life keeps declining.

According to US Census data, owner-occupied housing makes up less than 50% of all housing. Due to the low owner-occupied housing ratio, out-of-state property management businesses rent out over half of Ferguson's housing stock.

Additionally, the population has decreased from a little over 21,000 in 2010 to just over 18,000 in 2020.

It became dangerous to live and work in Ferguson. It can be dangerous to photograph protests, particularly in Ferguson. A protester may turn against the police, the media, or another protester.

To cover the George Floyd protests, I had to operate covertly. As a result, I avoided attending protests and instead focused on reporting on the fallout the next day. I also refrained from using a professional camera, opting instead to use my iPhone. I could move around the community discreetly because I didn't have professional camera equipment, which would make me stand out.

SPEED
LIMIT
25
WELCOME TO
FERGUSON

BLM
UNITED STATES POSTAL SERVICE
UNITED STATES POST OFFICE
MISSOURI

CHINESE Gourmet
RESTAURANT 522-0026
OPEN SUNDAY
BLACK Lives MATTER
INFINITI

TH
HOPE
LOVE
LOVE
Covington Connection
Your New Home
Beatrice C. Covington
314-709-7262
BLOS
BLACK
LIVES
MATTER

299
Symbols
in
all commun
OVE

POLICE DEPARTMENT
MUNICIPAL COURT
POLICE DEPARTMENT
MUNICIPAL COURT

BLM

DUO
Peruvian
Bundle Hair

Peruvian
Bundle Hair
5 pcs
1 PACK Solution

free

SOFT & SMOOTH TEXTURE
NEW HIGH TECH BLEND
LOOKS AND FEELS SO CLOSE TO HEALTHY HUMAN HAIR
SECURE DOUBLE-TRACK WEFT FOR A SUPERIOR FINISH
HEAT-FRIENDLY WITH GREAT CURL RETENTION

DUO
Bank

QUALITY
FOR THE MOST VALUE!

pur

NO PARKING
H2K
STYLE NO: SUNNY
COLOR: SILVER
SILVER

Quiznos
OPEN

INSTANT CROWD
PLEASERS
Slow-Roasted
PRIME RIB

Black
Owned
Please do not destroy

#BlackLives Matter
This is a Black
OWN DANCE Studio
This the KidS Happy Place
PLease Do NoT
#JusticeforFloyd
DESTROY OR Touch

307
BUSINESS
BLACK
OWNED

BLACK
OWNED

Black Owned
Business

KEEP
CALM
AND
PRAY
ON
BLACK
OWNED

KEEP
CALM
AND
PRAY
ON
LOVE
BRINGS
US
TOGETHER
BLACK OWNED

GOD COVERED
BLACK
OWNED
BLK

CATHY'S KITCHEN
love will win
@c7_look
BLACK OWNED BUSINESS
A

OPEN FOR BUSINESS
#BLACKLIVESMATTER BLACK OWNED
PARKING

WE ARE BLACK
FAMILY OWNED
BUSINESS

STAIRWAY
NO PARKING
PARKING IN REAR
PAWSITIVE
VIBES
grooming
314 712 9700
14
BLACK
LIVES
MATTER

RESIDENTS
LIVE
HERE
WE STAND WITH YOU
IN SOLIDARITY

City of Ferguson
POLICE DEPARTMENT
MUNICIPAL COURT

PRayer
Station
ALL
Welcome
INSIDE
FLOWERS
Jones
2020

This ignited smoke canister was discovered near the police station on S. Florissant Rd. in Ferguson this morning. The 40mm riot smoke projectile 4233. It has an 80-yard range.

The word "riot" appears in the product name. It doesn't say anything about "protest" or "unrest." However, "riot" is what Ferguson is dealing with, again, six years after Michael Brown. The city, and specifically the police department, is being held accountable for an unrelated incident that occurred 560 miles away.

4231
40MM RIOT CS SMOKE
MULTI-PROJECTILE (
(RANGE - 80YD (75 METER)
CTS
CLS COMBINED TACTICAL SYSTEMS
COMBINED 388 KINSMAN ROAD
TACTICAL SYSTEMS JAMESTOWN, PA 16134

Jones
2020
RONNIE
HARGE

Milk on the sidewalk the morning after a confrontation between police and demonstrators on South Florissant Road in the downtown area of Ferguson, Missouri, in the United States.

When poured into the eyes and applied to the skin, milk relieves the burning sensation caused by pepper spray and tear gas. Demonstrators discovered this information following the shooting of Michael Brown in 2014. It was standard practice for protestors to establish first-aid areas distant from the actual demonstration in order to treat persons who had been either directly sprayed with pepper spray or had become trapped in an area where tear gas was being distributed.

PARADISE
NOW!

FUCK 12! ALL DAY

CANTINA
OPEN

BLACK LIVES
MATTER,
FUCK TRUMP!

City of Ferguson
POLICE DEPARTMENT
MUNICIPAL COURT
HOPE

City of Ferguson
POLICE DEPARTMENT
MUNICIPAL COURT
CITY OF FERGUSON
POLICE DEPARTMENT
FTP

STOP
KILLER
COPS

City of Ferguson
POLICE DEPARTMENT
MUNICIPAL COURT
City of Ferguson
POLICE DEPARTMENT
MUNICIPAL COURT

Ella Jones 2020
FERGUSON PLAZA

HOW'S EVERYBODY
DOING ON S. CLAY?

R. Clay
HOW'S EVERYONE DOING ON·CHURCH ST?

HOW'S EVERYONE
DOING ON MAPLE ?

HOW'S EVERYONE
DOING ON ALMEDA ?

HOW'S EVERYBODY DOING ON N. CLAY?
St. Steph
BUIL
JOIN
ST
SAI
CHURCH

Ferguson
True Value
Hardware
GOING OUT OF BUSINESS
SALE 40% OFF

Hardware
Electrical
Plumbing
FOR SALE
8,070 +/- SQ FT
RETAIL BUILDING
HILLIKER
(314)
CORPORATION
781-0001

The
Teakwood Shop
FAMILY
HAIR STYLING
119
521-8500
117
BUSINESS IS
CLOSED
FOR
RETIREMENT
THANKS FOR
55 +
YEARS of
BUSINESS!!
Closed

Walgreens
Walgreens
Walgreens
PHARMACY
PHARMACY

FERGUSON OPTICAL
FOR SALE
4,530 +/- SF
BUILDING
POTENTIAL FOR THREE TENANTS
HILLIKER
(314)
CORPORATION
781-0001

About Steve Pellegrino

Documentary photographer Steve Pellegrino saw Ferguson, Missouri, from a different angle. As a 26-year resident, Steve was present from the start, unlike other photographers who traveled to Ferguson from other places to document the protests and violence.

Steve spent six years documenting the city's decline at the hands of outside activists and locals' and city authorities' efforts to make improvements.

His images from the 2014 Ferguson, Missouri protests were featured by prominent news magazines and media sources such as The Wall Street Journal, The Economist, Newsweek, Reason, NY Post, Deutsche Welle, and The Miami Herald.

Former Ferguson Chief of Police Thomas Jackson picked Steve as the sole photographic contributor to the book "Policing Ferguson, Policing America." Shelby Steele's award-winning documentary on racism in America, "What Killed Michael Brown?" incorporates his Ferguson photographs.

Following in the footsteps of many of their neighbors, Steve and his wife left Ferguson in 2021 and moved to a rural community in the Southwest.

www.ingramcontent.com/pod-product-compliance
Lightning Source LLC
Chambersburg PA
CBHW040301240726
48664CB00006B/1336